MINDFUL DEFENSIVE DRIVING

By

Gerald A. Hamel

TM

CONGRATULATIONS!

This retired Administrative Law Judge and Defensive Driving Instructor is pleased to welcome you and your willingness to investigate driving techniques that will enable you to belong to a unique group of people. Mindful people that have chosen to learn, implement and make a lifesaving habit of applying one's attention to defensive mindful driving. These are our goals:

1. To Be the BEST Mindful Defensive Drivers in the world.
2. Protect others and ourselves.
3. Save time and money.

It's a win-win situation. Keep reading.

"OUR LIVES DEPEND ON IT!"

CONTENTS

PROFESSIONAL AND EDUCATIONAL EXPERIENCE

- Completed Post-Graduate Studies for a Master's Degree in Counseling Psychology, John F. Kennedy University
- BA in Humanities, New College of California. American Bar Approved Paralegal Certificate, Saint Mary's College.
- Appointed by the Director of the California Department of Motor Vehicles into the position of an Administrative Law Judge (Hearing Officer), Driver Safety Division. Retired.
- Professional Paralegal/Legal Assistant for private law firms and governmental agencies.
- Past State of California licensed owner, operator and instructor for Alameda and Santa Cruz Traffic Schools. Current licensed traffic school instructor and Past licensed behind-the-wheel driving instructor.
- Completed the National Safety Council and the American Association of Retired People (AARP) Defensive Driving Courses.
- Conducts Seminars in Traffic Safety and Defensive Driving

INTRODUCTION

This book represents my method (Methodology) of teaching Defensive Driving with an emphasis on Mindfulness (awareness). It is my attempt to motivate you to learn, apply and make a habit out of becoming a Mindful Defensive Driver with the intent of saving lives. The forthcoming information is beneficial for any vehicle operator. *However, it is not intended to replace or be the primary source of information necessary to know in order to pass your examination for a driver's license or permit. Please check with your local governmental agencies to determine licensing requirements.*

You might say to yourself, "I'm a safe driver. Why do I need to read this?" Most people think they are good motor vehicle operators. The question I pose to you is this: Have you learned, implemented and made a driving habit out of formal defensive driving techniques or have you just been lucky? My experience suggests that the majority of drivers think they follow safe driving procedures but in reality they don't know, much less apply, defensive driving techniques.

After receiving my driver's license, and for many years thereafter, I considered myself a safe driver. If late for an event, I would cautiously drive faster to arrive on time as I was never taught time management procedures. I had a couple of traffic accidents that were deemed my fault but no one was injured or killed - doesn't everybody have a fender bender on occasion, I thought? My behavior gave little weight or consideration to the fact that my driving techniques and visual skills may have been the impetus that caused me to receive citations or cause my accidents. I was rationalizing my way to safety. My attitude changed after receiving a moving violation and subsequently attending traffic school.

The moving violation that changed my life: While following the flow of traffic while driving across the San Francisco Bay Bridge when suddenly a red light appeared in my rear view mirror. It was a California Highway Patrol officer. The speed limit was 50 miles per hour but everyone, including myself, was traveling around 60 miles per hour. Why me, I thought to myself as I safely negotiated my vehicle to the right side of the road and stopped. As the officer approached my vehicle, I looked him right in the eye and said, "Why me?" The officer looked me right in the eye and said, "Why not!" We both laughed as he was writing up my citation! The officer said, "Why don't you just go to traffic school?" I said, "That's a novel idea." As a result of receiving this citation, I attended traffic school and was delighted to have an instructor that really cared about saving lives through educating students on defensive driving techniques along with a review of traffic laws.

Prior to attending this class, I thought of myself as being a safe driver. As a result of attending this class, my perception shifted allowing me to become aware of the fact that my two accidents and past s speeding citations could have prevented. The instructor taught basic defensive driving techniques and I learned, applied and commenced making a habit out of this safer driving procedure. I am extremely grateful to say that I've been accident and moving violation free since attending this class. After the class ended, I approached the instructor, inquired how to become an instructor, became a licensed driving instructor in 1984, and commenced a life long journey teaching traffic safety.

I hope that the following presentation will motivate you to honestly examine your current driving methods; compare them to Mindful Defensive Driving Techniques and, if necessary, motivate you to change your driving habits.

INTRODUCTION TO CULTIVATING MINDFULNESS
Part One

Mindfulness means paying attention in the present moment in a non-judgmental manner. It does not conflict with any beliefs, traditions or religions as it merely increases our awareness and acceptance of the present moment. How many times have we arrived at our intended destination but don't remember what we experienced along the way? This is an example of being preoccupied with self while driving on "automatic pilot." We arrived at our destination without the ability to articulate what we experienced along the way. When driving on "auto-pilot," old driving habits will appear in response to particular driving situations thereby hindering our ability to operate our vehicle safely. Mindfulness represents an antidote to rote behavior, performing familiar, scripted actions without much cognition as if on autopilot.

By practicing and making a habit out of Mindful Defensive Driving Techniques coupled with cultivating mindfulness, we become more aware of the present moment, our thoughts, and our feelings. This will allow us to remember and articulate our driving experience and gives us greater freedom of choice in respect to reacting safely to any potential hazardous situations. More information on mindfulness along with specific exercises on how to cultivate mindfulness are included in this book.

WHAT IS YOUR DEFINITION OF A MINDFUL DEFENSIVE DRIVER

Take the following short quiz to determine if you are currently a Mindful Defensive Driver.

1. Do you always follow all traffic laws to the letter of the law?

2. How far ahead do you look when operating your vehicle?

3. How often do you look in the rear view mirror?

4. Should you continue glancing in your rear view mirror when stopped at a stop sign, stop light or any other time your vehicle is on the street and not in motion?

5. What procedure do you follow in order to make a safe right or left lane change?

6. What represents a safe distance between your vehicle and the vehicle directly in front of you?

7. List the things that other drivers do that really upset you.

8. How do you react to other driver's behaviors that make you upset or angry?

THE RESPONSIBILITY OF DRIVING

There is a huge responsibility behind driving a vehicle. A vehicle can be used as a weapon that can kill in an instant. It is essential that we buckle up, learn and apply not only defensive driving techniques, but mindful defensive driving techniques for the safety of ourselves and others. Are we always thinking about the tremendous amount of responsibility we have while operating a motor vehicle?

Do you think about what you're thinking about (metacognition)? Pertinent question. If so, what do we think about when we are operating a vehicle? Are we thinking, "Gee, I'm really going to be mindfully aware and practice defensive driving and follow all the traffic laws"? What do you think about when operating a motor vehicle? I'll come back to this idea in a moment but first let us consider the process of becoming a medical doctor.

8

How many years of education is required to become a medical doctor? Well, let's see. Pre-medical classes are required during the first four years of undergraduate work. How long is medical school? Four or five years and then a residency is required. A tremendous amount of education! After a medical student finally secures a medical license, they are required to complete additional coursework every year in order to maintain their license. Why? Because the position of a medical doctor includes a tremendous amount of responsibility, therefore, additional educational requirements are mandatory in order for them to keep abreast with new medications and medical techniques.

Most professionals that deal with the general public are required to seek and complete additional education on an annual basis. Doctors, attorneys, therapists, teachers, etc. Why? Because of the tremendous amount of *responsibility* they have in their chosen field.

After we receive our driver license, a responsible thing to have, how much more continuing education is required of us on an annual basis? None, unless the Department of Motor Vehicles requires additional training or an examination based on medical, physical or psychological reasons. Therefore, the only time we gain pertinent information to help keep us alive on the road (Defensive Driving Techniques) or have a review of traffic laws that we often forget, is when we receive a moving violation and choose to attend traffic school or gain it on our own – like reading this book.

HISTORY OF DEFENSIVE DRIVING

In 1952, Harold Smith established "The Smith System Driver Improvement Institute" and millions of drivers throughout the world have benefited from the program he developed (http://www.smith-system.com).

The most popular definition of Defensive Driving was developed in 1964 by the National Safety Council. The definition states that Defensive Driving is "driving to save lives, time, and money, in spite of the conditions around you and the actions of others (https://www.nsc.org) (ANSI/ASSE Z15).

The American Association of Retired People (AARP) has been involved in driver-improvement education since 1969, when AARP volunteers began teaching the Defensive Driving Course (DDC) of the National Safety Council. The DDC program was designed for all drivers age 16 and older. AARP was convinced that older drivers should have a training program of their own, so in 1979, they created one: AARP Driver Safety (then called "55 ALIVE"). The "55 ALIVE" program continued to teach defensive driving techniques but added information on age-related cognitive and physical changes that affect older drivers (http://www.aarp.org/home).

This author recognizes and appreciates any individual or organization that develops and communicates defensive driving and safety procedures in an attempt to keep us all safe. I propose, however, to expand upon the previously mentioned selected defensive driving techniques and include mindfulness in order to make us more aware thereby facilitating a safer driving environment. The object here is to encourage the reader to become aware of how you are operating a motor vehicle now, learn expanded ideas on defensive driving visual techniques, learn how to cultivate mindful driving through specific exercises and make a habit out of being a Mindful Defensive Driver.

THE PRINCIPLE OF MINDFUL DEFENSIVE DRIVING

What is a principle? Well, we have all heard of the Principle of Electricity. Who was that guy flying a kite with a key on the string that discovered electricity? Yes, Benjamin Franklin. He was lucky that he wasn't electrocuted! Benjamin Franklin discovered electricity. When we discover a natural law, we don't question why it is; we may never know "why it is." We just learn to use it. We can use electricity to heat our homes or we can use it to electrocute ourselves. Electricity doesn't care how we use it as it just is! It's not going to go over in the corner and cry if we fail to use it correctly—it just is! The principle of Mindful Defense Driving represents a principle liken to the Principle of Electricity. If we learn to use it correctly, it protects us (heats our homes,) but if we are ignorant of it or choose not to use its attributes, it can electrocute us.

For the benefit of ourselves, passengers in our vehicle and other vehicle operators and pedestrians, it would be a wise decision to choose to use the Principle of Mindful Defensive Driving constructively. It is our Choice! We are dealing with a principle that "has to work for us" as long as we are utilizing the principle correctly. The Principle of Mindful Defensive Driving consists of Two Standards and Four Elements:

STANDARD ONE: MINDFULLNESS AWARENESS

This section of the book articulates the definitions of mindfulness, awareness and self-consciousness in order to bring more clarity into the idea of Mindful Defensive Driving.

Modern day psychology defines Mindfulness as "bringing one's complete attention to the present experience on a moment-to-moment basis, paying attention in a particular way on purpose, in the present moment and non-judgmentally." An aim of mindfulness is to become grounded in the present moment. An important characteristic of mindfulness is awareness, "the state or ability to perceive, to feel, or to be conscious of events, objects, or sensory patterns." (Wikipedia.org) Awareness allows us to become conscious of our habitual reactions thereby allowing us to choose friendlier reactions associated with negative events that may occur while operating our vehicle on the streets and highways. For the intent of this book, mindfulness and awareness are interchangeable. Awareness may be confused with self-consciousness, "an acute sense of self-awareness or a preoccupation with oneself." (Wikipedia.org) Self-consciousness allows us to judge what we are experiencing against our opinions and image of ourselves. Here is an example of how it works. We are driving down a six-lane freeway, three lanes in each direction; a vehicle operator suddenly swerves into our lane almost causing a collision. The driver continues to change lanes, follows other vehicle operators too closely and is threatening their lives and the lives of others. Their behavior reflects their attitude about their safety and the safety of others. Perhaps they lack emotional maturity and respect for the safety of themselves and other drivers or maybe they are just having a bad day and simply don't care about themselves or others. We need to pay special attention to vehicle operators displaying this behavior.

Just as this driver cuts into our lane, we suddenly experience the feeling of fear and anger. If we are operating in the self-conscious mode (preoccupation with self), we may judge their behavior and feel justified in expressing a negative response. Perhaps we may seek revenge by teaching them a lesson like shouting at them,

13

catching up with them and following them too closely, or perhaps letting the bird out of the cage to express international sign language.

When anger rises, think of the consequences.

~ Confucius

As a Mindful Defensive Driver, we become mindful and aware of the presence of anger and fear within our self without judgment. This allows us a window of opportunity to react to the situation in a manner that will enhance the safety of all concerned. Perhaps you are thinking, "That's impossible to accomplish, other drivers don't give me the same courtesy, why should I extend this type of courtesy and understanding to them?" Why not? Our lives may depend on a conscious and compassionate response. We cannot control the behavior of other vehicle operators and pedestrians but we can control our reactions to them. As Mindful Defensive Drivers, we make every effort to stay in the moment while operating our vehicle and when negative events occur, we use our minds to react in a safe and sane manner. This is the essence of Mindful Defensive Driving. Additional information on how to cultivate Mindful Defensive Driving techniques are included in this book.

What is the opposite of mindfulness? Ellen J. Langer, PhD, a social psychologist at Harvard University, argues that people slip into a state of "mindlessness" by engaging in rote behavior, performing familiar, scripted actions without much cognition as if on autopilot. (http://susansmithjones.com)

What are we thinking about when we are driving? While operating a motor vehicle, most of us our thinking about getting to our destination; what we are planning for dinner this evening; the argument we just had with Aunt Mable at the family get together, etc. If we are thinking about all these ideas, who is doing the driving? Are we on autopilot? Perhaps that is exactly how we drive—on autopilot (i.e., rote behavior, performing familiar scripted actions without much cognition}. The driving methods taught to us when we initially learned how to drive our motor vehicle eventually turned into driving habits. Since we are habitual people, these habits eventually turned into what we may define as autopilot driving. In other words, autopilot is a result of our driving habits.

Who taught you how to drive a motor vehicle? Was it you parents, a relative, a friend, or perhaps you taught yourself? If taught by someone else, did they teach you defensive driving? If a professional driving instructor, or an instructor at a professional truck driving school teaches us, we may have been taught defensive driving techniques. More than likely, our driving mirrors the method taught to us by well-meaning people that may not have known Defensive Driving Techniques. Their teaching techniques, although well meaning, merely reflected the manner in which they learned how to drive. However, it may or may not represent defensive driving.

If we initially learned Defensive Driving, we would be aware of an emergency situation perhaps in time to avoid potential hazardous situations or fatal outcomes. After 30 plus years of teaching traffic school, I would estimate that approximately 80% of motor vehicle operators think they drive defensively but in fact are unaware of Defensive Driving Techniques.

"Don't learn safety by accident."
— Author Unknown

Mindful or Aware Defensive Driving means really paying attention to experiencing life in the "here and now."

HERE – NOW

We make every attempt to be present in the moment while operating any vehicle. For example: Prior to even entering our vehicle, we should take a few moments to STOP. What does STOP mean? It is an acronym that stands for the following:

S = STOP   T = Think   O = Observe   P = Proceed

Prior to operating our vehicle, we should take a few moments to merely relax; perhaps take a few deep breaths and simply become mindful (aware) of our breathing. This powerfully adjusts ourselves to the present moment. Prior to entering our vehicle, we may wish to walk around and inspect it or look at the tires to determine if additional air may be required. Do the windows need cleaning? Observe the vehicle's condition and look behind the vehicle for children and animals. Are there any children or animals present that may become a hazard? Observe your surroundings in and out of the vehicle.

When entering the vehicle, immediately secure your seat belt, check your mirrors, secure any object that may be loose enough to act as a missile if in a collision or a sudden stop, then look in the center mirror, look into your eyes and tell yourself you are preparing to drive now, "I follow Mindful Defensive Driving Techniques and the traffic laws, my life and the lives of others depend on my driving behavior."

Think about your destination. Perhaps check the news to determine if any accidents or traffic jams have occurred on your intended route. We "think" about the best route to use in order to get to our destination safely. In other words, prepare yourself to operate your vehicle. As Mindful Defensive Drivers, we don't merely enter our vehicle and take off. We S.T.O.P. (Stop, Think, Observe and Proceed). This procedure primes our mind to the idea of maintaining a continuous mindful attitude as we travel down the streets and highways together. It could save a life—perhaps your own.

The longest journey begins with a single step, not with a turn of the ignition key.
— Edward Abbey

Do you think it is important to be mindful (aware) of the things around us while operating a motor vehicle? Of course, the answer is yes! Our lives and the lives of others depend on it. Do you think that the majority of motor vehicle operators are fully aware of the things around them? What have you seen other drivers do that they should not be doing? How about holding a telephone to their ear while driving? In most states and perhaps nations, this action is illegal.

For those of us that have experienced an accident, we know that an accident occurs in a split second. We can't be on our phone and then tell the person we are talking to, "sorry I have to hang up, I'm currently having an accident". We should have both hands on the wheel at all times in order to make an evasive maneuver as quickly as possible. We do not have time to be talking on the phone.

We, as Mindful Defensive Drivers, are held to a higher standard than even the law itself. We simply choose not to talk on the phone. We either allow our phone to ring and take a message or have someone else answer it for us. What else have you seen other drivers do that they shouldn't be doing while driving?

How about eating while operating a vehicle? I like this one; people with a hamburger in one hand, a soft drink in the other, and they are driving with their legs and knees! I saw a person eating a salad the other day while driving— it's like they were in a restaurant. Again, we as Mindful Defensive Drivers do not eat or drink while driving. We are held to a higher standard. If we want to eat, we stop our vehicle first and then eat.

How about men shaving or women putting on their makeup? I notice this quite frequently. It's like our vehicles represent a bathroom with windows! Again, we as Mindful Defensive Drivers, simply do not engage in these sorts of activities while operating a motor vehicle. Remember, we are held to a higher standard.

What else have you noticed? How about reading while driving a motor vehicle? A number of years ago, a student told me that some motor vehicle drivers attach their lap top computers to their steering wheels and are typing while commuting to work! Again, we are held to a higher standard, we simply don't type while driving.

Being mindfully aware of everything around us while driving is absolutely essential if we want to survive the ride. Each and every time we get into our vehicle we are driving with all sorts of people under all sorts of situations. We are driving with drunks, drug addicts, drivers that fail to read the warning label on prescription medications, drivers that want to commit suicide and don't care if they take us with them, drivers that make up their own driving rules, drivers that may have serious mental problems, drivers that just broke up with their girl or boy friend, and even drivers that just died! Is there ever a time that we can just set back and relax while operating a vehicle? I mean we don't have to be all uptight and tense, but we must be vigilant, mindful, and aware at all times because <u>our lives and the lives of others depend on it.</u>

Part of the process of attending traffic school includes a segment where each and every student communicates with the class and shares what citation they received and how much it cost. One student had run right through a red light. I said, "Oh, you didn't see the red light?" Their answer was, "Yes, I saw the red light but it doesn't belong there." This student was serious! They could have been dead serious! This may be an isolated example of the types of drivers on the road but it only takes one driver like this student to kill us.

STANDARD TWO:

FOLLOWING THE TRAFFIC LAWS TO THE BEST OF OUR DRIVING ABILITY

Do we always follow the traffic laws perfectly? For example, do we always make a complete stop at the stop sign or do we sort of slide through it? What is the definition of stop? Can the vehicle's wheels be turning at all for a complete stop? The answer is no. We are required by traffic laws to completely stop our vehicle. The wheels should not be moving at all. We should feel the vehicle jerk back as we look to our left for oncoming traffic, such as pedestrians, bicyclists or anything that could impede our travel. Scan to the right and observe the same things then look forward. Look to our left again and, if safe, proceed with caution. That's the definition of a complete stop. Do we always stop in this manner? Well, if your answer is yes—good for you! Generally speaking, if we are truly honest with ourselves, many vehicle operators will admit that they stop in this manner some of the time but not all of the time. Why? Because we human beings are not perfect. We make mistakes.

According to the California Vehicle Code, a vehicle operator can make a right turn on a red light if we stop completely, yield to any oncoming vehicles and pedestrians, no sign prohibits it and it's safe.

I've had numerous students who received a photo-citation for running a red light on a right turn. They tell me they honestly believed that they came to a complete stop at the corner prior to negotiating their right turn. Most students argued their position until they went on the internet and viewed themselves actually running the red light. In California, as in probably most states, and perhaps nations, students can access videos that recorded their violation.

We are not perfect vehicle operators because we human beings are not perfect. However, the more we can discipline ourselves to make a complete stop prior to making a right turn or to follow all traffic laws to the best of our ability, the better off we are.

I'm not attempting to present a bunch of pie-in-the-sky platitudes that are impossible to obtain. <u>Mindful Defensive Driving represents an intelligent way to approach traffic safety</u>. It lends itself well to people who like to think. If you like to "think" about things, you will like this approach to traffic safety.

We use our minds to keep us alive.

Essentially, the more we can follow traffic laws, like completely stopping behind the line on a red light prior to negotiating our turn, the better off we are.

We are building up *habit patterns*. We want to get the numbers on our side. If we can drive mindfully most of the time, we will be driving more safely than most other drivers.

When teaching Defensive Driving I use a white board with markers. I write down the Two Standards then place four numbers (1, 2. 3. 4) on the board to represent the four elements. I ask the participants, and I'm asking the reader right now, do you believe that you are a defensive driver?

If your answer is yes, that's great! If your answer is no, or you don't know, that's good also, because according to my years of teaching experience, most drivers think they drive defensively but in reality the vast majority of vehicle operators simply have never been taught defensive driving techniques.

We cannot know and apply Mindful Defensive Driving Techniques unless we are taught or use common sense.

Do you think that most of us human beings have plain old common sense? Most of my students, when presented with this question, sort of raise their eyebrows indicating that some people have common sense but not all of us. How about Abe Lincoln's comment on common sense:

G.HAMEL

"Common sense is not so common"

We have all met very educated, intelligent people that don't display plain old common sense. Albert Einstein could figure out the mysteries of the Universe but had difficulties in other areas of his life as we all do. However, we have thumbs, therefore, we have the capacity to learn new ideas and apply them. With this in mind, let's take a look at the four essential elements of Mindful Defensive Driving to determine if we actually use common sense in our driving experience.

ESSENTIAL ELEMENT NUMBER 1: LOOKING AHEAD

When teaching Mindful Defensive Driving skills, I ask the students to think about how far ahead they look while operating their motor vehicle. Some will say that they look at the vehicle right in front of them. Some will respond by saying that they simply never thought about it. They are just looking forward. Many respond by saying that they look two to three vehicles ahead.

23

Question: If we are looking at the vehicle right in front of us, who is doing the driving?

We are placing our lives and trust on the person operating the vehicle in front of us. Are they a mindful driver? We don't know. We don't even know who they are. So...if we aren't supposed to be just looking at the vehicle in front of us, where else should we be looking?

The average driver looks from 2-3 vehicles in front of them.

We, as Mindful Defensive Drivers, are held to a higher standard, therefore, every few seconds we look as far ahead as possible. Of course, we are constantly scanning our environment but every few seconds we are looking ahead as far as possible.

Some experts say we should look at least one block ahead in a residential or business area and as far as possible on the freeway.

It is essential to develop a habit pattern of looking ahead as far as possible every few seconds at all times and in all locations while operating our vehicle.

In addition, we are always keeping our eyes moving, scanning our environment. We should look forward as far as possible, scan to the left then to the right, and then bring our vision back to the vehicles around us. We should check our rearview mirror and then start the process over and over again.

If the vehicle in front of us is blocking our view forward, we either position ourselves so we can see ahead or increase the following distance from the vehicle in front of us.

Why increase the following distance?

Because we don't know what's ahead of the vehicle in front of us, therefore, increasing the following distance gives additional time to react in time when confronted with an emergency situation. In addition, we attempt not to travel in the other vehicle's blind spot and we remember to communicate our intentions to other drivers.

There is a physiological reason why we need to continually scan our environment. We have two types of vision. We have direct vision and peripheral vision. If we stare at something longer then 3-4 seconds, we begin to lose or reduce our peripheral vision.

In order to compensate for the loss of our peripheral vision, we must continually keep our eyes moving by scanning our environment.

What are we looking for while scanning our environment?

Anything that may impede our direction of travel. For example, we are looking at moving and parked vehicles, pedestrians, animals, stop signs, stoplights, road signs, road markings and so forth.

The Streets Talk To Us

The streets are telling us their story in signs, symbols and colors. As we are moving forward, and continually scanning, we keep safe and in the present moment by being mindful of everything around us as we read the signs, symbols and colors of the road.

Business and Residential. Looking far ahead in this environment is extremely important because of all the potential hazards we face while operating our vehicle's in business and residential areas (i.e. other vehicle's, pedestrians, bicyclists, motorcycles, children, parked cars and trucks, etc.). Paying attention to traffic signals, signs and road line colors are particularly important in this environment. Furthermore, If we glance ahead as far as possible every few seconds while driving in this environment, it is highly unlikely that we will ever receive a citation for running a red light.

Freeway Driving. Every few seconds we should look ahead as far as possible while scanning our immediate environment. It is amazing to find out how many times one can avoid being stuck in traffic by merely noticing brake lights appearing far ahead.

This visual skill allows one to exit the freeway in a safe and timely manner. When noticing brake lights appearing farther ahead, emergency flashers can be engaged in order to warn other drivers of impending an emergency (don't forget to turn them off afterwards).

Every Few Seconds Scan Ahead As Far as Possible.
Check for Vehicles Around, Behind and In Your Blind
Spots. Check Rear View Mirror Every Few Seconds

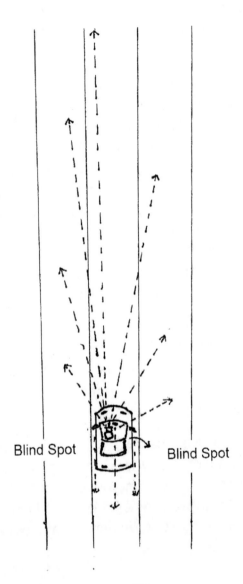

Blind Spot   Blind Spot

Your safety gears are between your ears.
— Author Unknown

Making Mindful Defensive Driving a habit enables us to anticipate potential problems, adjust our speed and predict what could possibly happen in accordance with our intelligent assessment of the situation. We don't react by getting emotional and thinking, "that truck shouldn't be in that location" or "why don't they hurry up and get out of the way." We merely are mindful and aware of the situation before us then react in accordance to our intelligent assessment of the situation.

The best car safety device is a rear-view mirror with a cop in it. — Dudley Moore

ESSENTIAL ELEMENT NUMBER 2: LOOKING BEHIND

We are driving forward so why all the fuss about looking in the rear-view mirror? Many students will respond to this question by saying, "We look for cops!" Well, there are other reasons why we are looking in our mirrors besides merely looking for police officers particularly check behind us when coming to a stop, as we don't want to be rear-ended. As Mindful Defensive Drivers, *we want to know what's around us at all times*. How often do you look in your rear-view mirror? How often do you think we should look in our rear-view mirror? The answer received from students range from, "I don't know" to "once in a while" to "every 5-10 minutes" to "it depends on where I'm driving" to "every couple of minutes" to "whenever I think I need to look."

We should make a habit out of glancing in our review-view mirrors every few seconds and even more frequently if conditions warrant it – like when driving down a busy city street. It is essential to incorporate this procedure even while completely stopped at a stop sign or red light. Why? Because we want to know what is all around us <u>at all</u> <u>times</u> even when stopped. Our lives and the lives of others depend on it. Just remember to glance in your rear-view mirror every few seconds at all times. Driving forward, we should be looking as far as possible every few seconds, and looking in our rear-view mirror every few seconds. We want to make a habit out of this procedure. Yes. <u>A Habit</u>!

Do you think that we human beings are creatures of "Habit"? I observe that we are big-time creatures of habit. Think about it. Didn't we basically do the same thing this morning as we did yesterday morning and the morning before that? Generally, we do not change our life habit patterns unless we are forced to change them. Who taught you how to operate a vehicle? Was it your father, mother, a relative or friend? Did they teach you Mindful Defensive Driving skills? More than likely, they taught you their techniques for operating a vehicle. Did their teaching methods include the contents of this book? What driving habits did you develop after being taught how to drive?

Aristotle

We are what we repeatedly do; excellence, then, is not an act but a habit. — Aristotle

The way we learned how to operate a vehicle eventually turned into driving habit patterns. Therefore, the driving method we currently use represents our driving habits. If the person that initially taught you how to operate a vehicle taught you defensive driving skills, those skills represent your driving habits and this book merely represents a review for you. If you didn't learn these skills, this book represents a new, mindful, safer way to operate your vehicle.   With increased awareness (mindfulness), we have additional responsibilities. We can never say that we don't know about Mindful Defensive Driving Techniques. Now that we have this information, how do we incorporate it into our current driving experience? How long does it take to change our old driving habits and replace them with new driving habits?

According to Susan Smith, PhD, it takes 21 days of consistently repeating an activity before your mind accepts it as a habit (http:susansmithjones.com). Some experts say that it may take 60 or more days to change habit patterns. Perhaps it's all up to the individual how long it takes to formulate a new habit pattern. For the average person, it should take approximately 21 to 30 days to change habit patterns. Based on this assumption, for a 21 day investment, we will be on our way to becoming one of the *best Mindful Defensive vehicle operators in the world.*

21
DAYS to Change a Habit

Food for thought: What is the main attribute that is absolutely essential in respect to reaching any goal that we set in life? Is it not self-discipline? We are required to make ourselves mind ourselves if we truly desire to accomplish any goal. This is true if we want a higher education or if we desire to be a professional, tradesman or go into sports. Any endeavor we wish to accomplish requires self-discipline. Why not discipline ourselves to learn, implement and make Mindful Defensive Driving skills our driving habits. What's the result? Life and the possibility of having an accident-free driving record. It's a winning combination.

We are all in this together and by learning and implementing Mindful Defensive Driving Techniques, we become part of the solution instead of part of the problem. When we belong to the best drivers in the world club, our chances of reaching all other life goals will increase because we will be alive to obtain them. Sometimes my behind-the-wheel driving students say, "Why do you want me to drive like an older person"? My response to students that ask this question is "They got old, didn't they"? Getting to be an older person is a privilege denied to many."

Working safely may get old, but so do those who practice

it. — Author Unknown

If we actually make the effort to take a mere 21 days to learn, implement and make Mindful Defensive Driving skills a habit, will our efforts guarantee us that we will never experience an accident? Of course not. We don't have any control over a drunk driver that runs into our vehicle. What it means, however, is that if we are in an accident, it is highly likely that we will walk away from it while the other guy may die, unfortunately. We are seriously talking about life and death issues.

Better a thousand times careful than once dead. — Proverb

ESSENTIAL ELEMENT NUMBER 3: BLIND SPOT (S.M.O.G.)

Say we are driving down a three-lane freeway and decide to make a right lane change. What procedure do you follow in order to negotiate a safe right lane change? Have you heard of the acronym S.M.O.G.? This stands for Signal, Mirror, Over-the-shoulder, and Go. It is essential for us to look over our shoulder prior to making a lane change or times when we need to be mindful (aware) of other vehicles around us. Our lives and the lives of others depend on it. We have all experienced times when we almost collided with another vehicle because they were in our Blind Spot.

S. M. O. G.

S = Smog
M = Mirrors
O = Over the Shoulder
G = Go

1. SIGNAL
2. MIRRORS
3. LOOK OVER YOUR RIGHT SHOULDER
4. GO (IF SAFE)

Right Lane Change - Reverse Procedure for Left Lane Change

I always tell students to watch out for their B.S. because it can get them or someone else killed. I mean Blind Spot of course.

Exactly what constitutes our Blind Spot?

The following represents an exercise we can use to determine exactly where the Blind Spot is located on our particular vehicle. Take your vehicle along with a friend to a safe area with a lot of room around you (Perhaps a large empty parking lot). Place your vehicle in an area

33

with lots of room around it. Have your friend bring some markers with them like a book, rag, or a can. Any object will work that can be used to place a marker in a specific location around your vehicle.

Sit behind the wheel in your vehicle and have your friend position themselves right in front of your vehicle on the driver's side. It is good to have the vehicle stationary during this time! Your friend is facing you and you're looking at them. Have your friend slowing back up until you can see your friend's shoes or feet. Honk your horn and have your friend place a marker on the ground where they stand.

Once this is accomplished, have your friend stand right outside the driver's side door and window and have your friend slowly back up until you can see their feet. Honk your horn and have your friend place the second marker on the ground in that location. At this point, your friend should walk around to the rear of the vehicle and position themselves on the right side of the vehicle. Look out your rear-view mirror (not your side mirrors) and, once again, have your friend slowly move backwards until their shoes or feet appear in your rear-view mirror. Honk your horn when you see their feet and, once again, they will place a marker on the ground in that location. Next, have your friend position themselves right outside the front passenger door. Once again, they will slowly move away from the door horizontally and when you can see their feet, peep your horn and have them place a marker in that location.

After all the markers are in position, get out of your vehicle and walk around the markers. The ground within the markers around your vehicle is considered our blind spot. When we are positioned in our vehicle, we cannot see the ground within those markers. This constitutes our blind spot. This will give us a better idea of just how important it is to always look over our shoulders prior to changing lanes, making turns and any other time that we must determine where other vehicles are located around us. I always tell new driving students that it is essential that they remember this rule because they can get killed or kill someone else if they fail to remember this rule.

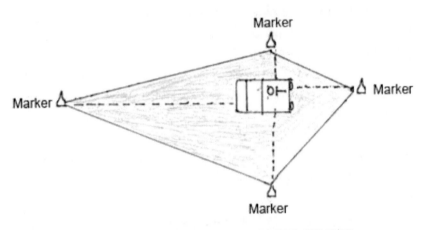

SHADED AREA = BLIND SPOTS

Now that you know what your blind spot represents, what do you think represents the blind spot on a semi-truck? It's huge! There is a large blind spot in the front and along the sides as well as a substantial blind spot in the rear of the truck. This fact establishes our position that it is not wise to travel alongside a truck if we can possibly help it. We either accelerate and go past it or take our foot off the accelerator and fall behind it. Generally there is a sign located on the truck that warns us, "If you can't see the truck driver in their mirror, they can't see you." Did you hear about the little Volkswagen that cut right in front of a truck and had to suddenly stop? It became a bug!

Visual technique for lane changing: Consider the following visual skills the next time you're traveling on the freeway, pass a semi-truck, or any other truck or vehicle, and want to move into their lane of travel safely.

Never, ever negotiate a lane change until you pass the vehicle in the lane you wish to enter, look in your center rear-view mirror and are able to see the <u>lights and tires</u> of the vehicle located in the lane you wish to enter. Check to determine if the vehicle traveling in the lane you wish to enter is moving up on you and check out other drivers that may be anticipating a similar lane change. Then you can safely move into your lane of choice. Perhaps we could enter the lane safely prior to seeing a truck's lights and tires—however, if the vehicle traveling in the same lane as we are suddenly stops, we may be able to stop in time to avoid hitting the forward vehicle but we may be rear-ended by the truck. That would ruin our day! Do you know how much a fully loaded semi-truck weighs? About 80,000 pounds! Our vehicle's generally weigh about 2,000 to 4,000 pounds.

One of the main complaints from truck drivers reflects the fact that other drivers pull in front of them too quickly.

The truck driver doesn't want to hit us, they simply can't help it because of their truck's weight factor. Therefore, we must watch out for them. In conclusion to this section remember the following: Always watch out for your B.S. - it can get you or someone else killed. I mean Blind Spot, of course.

While conducting Defensive Driving Seminars, the following question is asked the students: "What represents a safe distance between our vehicle and the vehicle in front of us?" The answers vary. Some students simply don't know the answer because they are not mindful (aware) of their distance. This is an important response to fully grasp. Why? Because when a driver is tailgating us (following our vehicle too closely) they may not be cognitive of the dangers they present. Understanding this fact allows us to be more levelheaded and not get upset with tailgaters. Other students will answer by indicating that as long as they can see the tires on the vehicle in front of them they are at a safe distance. What do you think is a safe distance?

ESSENTIAL ELEMENT NUMBER 4: DISTANCE

The distance between our vehicle and the vehicle in front of us varies according to our speed. In good weather conditions, we should be traveling at one car length for every 10 miles per hour. If we are traveling 30 miles per hour, the distance is 3 car lengths, if traveling 60 miles per hour, the distance would be 6 car lengths. The faster we go, the further away we distance ourselves. Is this rule written in cement? Of course not. Here are some examples of when we would increase our distance from the vehicle in front of us:

When being tailgated. If we were unable to move into another lane or pull to the side allowing the tailgater to pass us, we would increase our distance. Why? Because if we have to stop suddenly we need to allow extra room to stop in order to avoid being rear-ended by the vehicle behind us. Driving on slippery roads, following motorcyclists, towing a trailer, following large vehicles or merging onto a freeway may warrant our decision to follow from a safer distance. If it's at night, following a truck or camper or the road conditions are bad, we would follow from an even greater distance.

How far represents a car length? Are we talking about a large vehicle or a small vehicle? How many car lengths does a semi-truck represent? How can we tell three or six car lengths? That's a hard one to figure out, therefore, it's a general rule that we estimate what 3 car lengths may represent. There is another method we can us to keep us safe. It is called the 3-Second Rule.

The 3-Second Rule states that in good weather and conditions we should be following the vehicle in front of us by 3 seconds. This distance would increase to 4 seconds or more when driving at night, in bad weather, when following a truck or other vehicle that hinders our ability to see ahead at a safe distance, or any other condition that challenges our ability to drive safely.

One Car Length for Every 10 Miles per Hour = 3 Second Rule Under Ideal Conditions

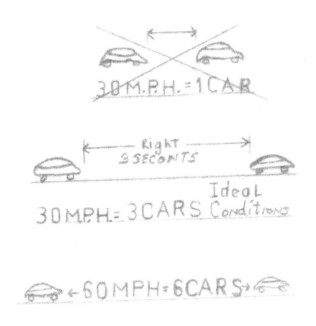

30 M.P.H. = 1 CAR

30 MPH = 3 CARS   Right 3 SECONTS   Ideal Conditions

← 60 MPH = 6 CARS →

How do we determine if we are following a vehicle by 3 seconds? As we are traveling down the streets and highways together, we look forward and choose a stationary object that we will eventually pass. It could be a tree, a telephone pole, or a large rock   When the vehicle in front of us passes our chosen object, we begin to count "one thousand one, one thousand two, and one thousand three." If our vehicle passes the same chosen object when we reach one thousand three, we are 3 seconds behind the vehicle in front of us.

What should we do if the vehicle in front passes our chosen object and we count to ourselves "one thousand one" and then immediately pass the object? We would take our foot off the accelerator thereby slowing our vehicle down and then choose another stationary object ahead of us and continue the process until we reach "one thousand three."

Another example: It's a beautiful day. The sun is shining and the birds are singing. We are traveling down a six lane freeway (three lanes in each direction) and notice a freeway overpass ahead of us. The sun is shining down on the freeway overpass and a shadow appears under the freeway. We will use that shadow as our chosen, fixed object. Once, a student remarked, "a shadow isn't a fixed object!" My response was, "that's correct but the shadow moves slowly, therefore, we can use it." As the vehicle in front of us passes the shadow (the moving fixed object), we start to count "one thousand one, one thousand two, and one thousand three." If our vehicle passes the freeway overpass shadow when we reach one thousand three, we are three seconds behind the vehicle in front of us. Again, if the count is interrupted, we take our foot off the accelerator, slow down and choose another fixed object until we reach "one thousand three."

This procedure reflects a mechanical way of developing an intuitive sense of what the three seconds represent. After practicing this procedure a few times, we will intuitively sense when we are 3 seconds behind a vehicle. Remember, the 3 second rule is followed under ideal conditions. We use our intelligent assessment of the situation in order to determine our course of action.

If we actually learn, implement and make a habit out of the 3 or more second rule, what will occur periodically? Most students respond by saying it's impossible to follow the 3 second rule because other drivers will constantly cut in front of us forcing us to back off. This does occur, but remember we are following a principle that has to work as long as we are applying it correctly. When someone enters our lane, what do we do? We back off. We don't have to give them international sign language or anything like that, we merely back off and resume our safe distance. If another vehicle enters again, we follow the same procedure. If another vehicle enters our lane of travel, we continue to follow the same procedures and if they enter again, we drive home and take the bus because we are never going to get to our destination! Ha! Think about the following:

How many times have you been traveling down the freeway only to notice the driver of the vehicle ahead changing lanes and following everybody too closely? The person driving recklessly may think that their driving actions are facilitating an early arrival to his or her destination. Is this true? Of course not. They are simply practicing dangerous driving maneuvers and are endangering their lives and the lives of everyone around them. It's all in their head! Because of their irresponsible driving habits or their lack of knowledge about defensive driving techniques, they may not arrive at their destination. In reality, the way we operate our vehicle reflects our driving habits and tells the whole world how we feel about our own safety and the safety of others. Since it is impossible to drive through the vehicle in front of us, it is pure common sense to drop back and travel at a safe distance. We increase our chances of arriving safely to our destination and protect ourselves and other drivers at the same time. It's a winning situation.

"It's good to have an end in mind but in the end what counts is how you travel." — Orna Ross

CULTIVATING MINDFULNESS Part Two

Mindfulness means paying attention in the present moment in a non-judgmental manner. It does not conflict with any beliefs, traditions or religions as it merely increases our awareness and acceptance of the present moment. How many times have we arrived at our intended destination but don't remember what we experienced along the way. This is an example of being preoccupied with "self" while driving on "automatic pilot." We arrive at our destination without the ability to articulate what we experienced along the way. When driving on "auto-pilot," old driving habits will appear in response to particular driving situations thereby hindering our ability to operate our vehicle safely. Mindfulness represents an antidote to rote behavior, performing familiar, scripted actions without much cognition as if on autopilot.

By practicing and making a habit out of Mindful Defensive Driving Techniques coupled with cultivating mindfulness, we become more aware of the present moment, our thoughts, and our feelings. This will allow us to remember and articulate our driving experience and gives us greater freedom of choice in respect to reacting safely to any potential hazardous situations.

The main method used to cultivate mindfulness is concentration and meditation. Concentration facilitates mindful attention. Of course, we are not going to literally practice meditation while operating our vehicle but the practice of meditation will facilitate increased awareness in respect to our ability to be safer vehicle operators. However, it is not necessary to practice meditation in order to become a Defensive Driver.

If we simply practice the principle of Mindful Defensive Driving with its Two-Standards and Four Essential Elements for 21 days, we will most certainly become safer drivers. In order to increase our ability to be fully Mindful Defensive Drivers, I suggest that you make a decision to take a few moments out of your day to practice some form of concentration or meditation.

There are different definitions of meditation or concentration. For example, when reading a book our minds may be totally focused in the present moment. When engaged in any form of art like music, oil or watercolor painting, dancing, for examples, we practice a form of meditation or concentrated effort in the present moment. Therefore, there may be many definitions to the idea of meditation. Cultivating mindfulness will allow more awareness of the present moment which includes being conscious of our thoughts and feelings while operating a vehicle. This will enable us to be more fully present while driving and allow us the opportunity to react to potential hazards consciously instead of reacting on automatic pilot. A trained mind far excels an untrained mind.

The following represents a couple of short five to ten minute exercises that we can use to develop more mindfulness.

Mindfulness Exercise # 1 — Breath

1. Sit in a chair with your back straight and feet planted fully on the floor. 2. Close your eyes and become aware of your breath as it enters and leaves your body. Become conscious of how your diaphragm raises and lowers as your breath goes in and out of your body.

3. The second you become aware that you are thinking or feeling emotions about a particular situation, concentrate on bringing your thoughts or emotions back

to your breath and the raising and lowering of your diaphragm. That's it. Pretty simple, isn't it?

4.   After completing this exercise for 5-10 minutes, you may feel more focused in the present moment. Keep in mind that it takes a minimum of 21 days to create a new habit pattern in the subconscious mind, therefore, give yourself some time to more fully cultivate mindfulness.

Mindfulness Exercise # 2 — Emotions

1.   Sit in a chair with your back straight and feet planted fully on the floor.

2.   Close your eyes and become aware of your breath as it enters and leaves your body. Become conscious of how your diaphragm raises and lowers as your breath goes in and out of your body.

3.   Say, for example, you start to feel uncomfortable anger emotions over someone that has upset you. You may notice that your body starts to get more rigid and perhaps your breath is shallower. The second you become aware of the emotion, concentrate on bringing your attention back to the present moment by concentration on your breath and the rising and falling of your diaphragm (stomach). If the emotion continues, the minute you become aware of the negative emotion, commence thinking about a time when you experienced joy and happiness. Experience your body posture and breathe changes. Your body may become more relaxed and your breath comes back to normal.

Mindfulness Exercise # 3 — In the Moment

In this exercise, we practice a running narrative with ourselves. We internally verbalize what behavior we are experiencing in the moment. For example, when we walk to our vehicle, we may say to yourself, "I'm now walking around my vehicle; do I have everything I need for my journey"? I'm looking behind the vehicle to check for children, animals or other objects." Just prior to entering our vehicle, we may say, "I'm now entering my vehicle, closing the door, positioning my mirrors and am now taking a deep breath and relaxing. I'm placing the key in the ignition and starting my vehicle, looking in the mirrors and observing everything around me prior to backing out of the garage or entering the street. I look in the mirror and remind myself that I'm a Mindful Defensive Driver. This may assist us in staying present in the moment and may enhance mindfulness.

Mindfulness Exercise # 4 — Relaxing

Deep Breathing: We can lie down or sit in a chair in this exercise. Place your hands on the lower part of your stomach. Concentrate on your breath and notice how your hands rise as you slowly inhale. Gently push your stomach with your hands as you exhale and repeat the process for whatever time you desire. You can also conduct an inner dialogue with yourself. Try to imagine tension and stress leaving your body as you exhale and peace and relaxation entering your body as you inhale. This is another method of keeping us present in the here and now therefore facilitating the process of being mindful.

These simple methods of meditation allow us to more fully cultivate mindfulness and allow us the opportunity to maintain awareness and control over our thoughts and emotions. Are we going to dedicate ourselves to practice on a daily basis the above-mentioned exercises? Some people practice 5-10 minutes a day initially and some may practice 30 minutes to an hour. Whatever time we allow practicing concentration and meditation, the more mindful and aware we will become as we operate our vehicles.

If you miss practicing for a day or more, don't get discouraged because no one is judging or keeping a record. Making a decision to dedicate ourselves to actually practicing the above-mentioned exercises on a daily basis is similar to our decision to practice the traffic laws to the best of our ability — the second standard in Defensive Driving. We as human beings are not perfect but the more we can follow the traffic laws the better off we will be. We want to get the safety numbers on our side and increase our concentration and mindfulness.

The more we can cultivate concentration and some sort of meditation on a daily basis, the more mindful we will become while operating our vehicle. We will have more control over our thoughts and emotions thereby allowing us the opportunity to react to hazardous driving situations in a sane, emotionally mature and mindful manner.

How do we apply this exercise to driving mindfully? Remember the vehicle operator that swerved into our lane while driving on the 6-lane freeway? Our immediate reaction could be that of anger and fear based on an automatic pilot perspective. We may lose control over our thoughts and emotions and try to get revenge. As Mindful Defensive Drivers, we would take a deep breath, quickly acknowledge the feeling of fear and anger within ourselves but not react to the fear and anger. We would merely acknowledge it, perhaps take a breath, and choose to maintain safe driving behavior. Cultivating mindfulness will improve our ability to think before we act thereby promoting a safer driving environment for our lives and the lives of others.

Life is 10% what happens to me and 90% of how I react to it.— Charles Swindoll

Please note: It is unsafe to practice *formal* meditation or be involved in any other activity that would hinder our ability to drive safely while operating our vehicle.

REVIEW AND ANSWERS TO BEGINNING QUIZ

What is your definition of a mindful, aware vehicle operator? Answer: By now you have the answer.

1. Do you always follow all traffic laws to the letter of the law? Answer: In general, the answer is no because we human beings are not perfect.

However, the more we do follow traffic laws to the letter of the law, the better off we are. We want to get the numbers on our side – tip the scale of safety into our favor. By following the traffic laws to the best of our ability, we generate positive driving habits that can quite literally save lives, injuries and property.

2. How far ahead do you look when operating your vehicle? Answer: Every few seconds we should look as far ahead as possible. If following a vehicle that blocks our view ahead, we either change lanes or position our vehicle so we can see ahead or we increase our following distance.

3. How often do you look in the rear view mirror? Answer: Every few seconds at all times.

4. Should you continue glancing in your rear-view mirror when stopped at a stop sign, stop light or any other time your vehicle is on the street and not in motion? Answer: Yes. We want to know what is around us at all times.

5. What procedure do you follow in order to make a safe right or left lane change? Answer: S.M.O.G. Signal, Mirror, Over the shoulder in the direction of travel and Go – if safe.

6. What represents a safe distance between your vehicle and the vehicle directly in front of you? Answer: Three seconds or one car length for every ten miles per hour under ideal conditions.

Increase your distance under less than ideal conditions.

7. List the things other motor vehicle operators do that upset you. Answer: Look at your answers. Does any of your own driving habits reflect similar behavior patterns? In psychology it's called projection. We project upon others what we don't like about ourselves. This is a method for self-examination.

8. How do you react to other driver's behaviors that make you upset or angry? Answer: Learn and apply Mindful Defensive Driving in order to reduce anxiety and increase your ability to react in a calm, intelligent and mindful manner.

SUMMARY OF MINDFUL DEFENSIVE DRIVING

The principle of Mindful Defensive Driving is likened to the principle of electricity. We can use electricity to heat our home or to electrocute us. It doesn't care how we use it. The principle of Mindful Defensive Driving is the same. If we learn to use it constructively, it works for us (heats our home). If we are ignorant of it or we choose to disregard it, it works against us (electrocutes us). With increased awareness (mindfulness) comes increased responsibility. For a 21-day investment, we can change our current driving habits into Mindful Defensive Driving Techniques. The results of utilizing this method enables us the opportunity to be the best drivers in the world; we protect ourselves, we protect others, and we save money. The Principle of Mindful Defensive Driving consists of two standards and four essential elements:

Standard One: Being Mindful (Aware)

Standard Two: Following the traffic laws as much as humanly possible.

Element One: Looking ahead every few seconds as far as you can while scanning to the left and the right; forward and back to the vehicle in front of you.

Element Two: Blind Spot: When changing lanes and making turns, we always follow the acronym SMOG: Signal, Mirror, Over the Shoulder, and Go!

Element Three: Following Distance. In good weather and conditions, follow a minimum of three seconds. One car length for every ten miles per hour. At night, when it's raining, snowing, etc. we following at a greater distance.

Element Four: Looking Behind every few seconds even when stopped. Looking behind, looking behind, looking behind – and we want to make a *HABIT* out of all Mindful Driving Techniques. How long does it take to change one habit with another habit? 21 Days! How much does it cost? It costs no money—it's Free. The only cost is making a conscious Choice to apply the Principle of Mindful Defensive Driving Techniques for 21 days. Our success will grant us membership into a unique group of people who:

1. Our considered The BEST Drivers in the World.
2. Protect themselves and other people around us
3. Save money.

What is the end result?   LIFE – that is a pretty good deal. Aren't' you glad you read this book!

ACKNOWLEDGEMENTS

My first acknowledgement and thanks go to Irenee Riter for her hours of assistance and excellent guidance in respect to publishing this book. Many thanks for her generosity and expertise.

Early drafts of this book were read and edited by Diana Bond. Joan Tavares read and gave valuable feedback and support and Maria Martinez Wong converted some illustrations. Later editing was done by Cyndy Patrick. I am extremely grateful to everyone who contributed to making this book possible.

Finally, but certainly not least, I want to express my deep gratitude and respect to all the students that have attended a traffic school class taught by me. Your valuable comments, opinions and insights about how everyone should know defensive driving techniques in order to save lives and keep us out of accidents was and is the inspiration behind writing this book.

With the exception of Doodlers from driving class, all Illustrations were completed by the author.

Testimony

When I was in high school, we never had Drivers Ed in school. It wasn't until I had an accident that I had to go to drivers' school to get the accident taken off my record. I learned so much from that course that I wasn't even aware of. And I haven't had an accident since that time except when someone ran into me. Jerry's class points out that you don't pull out to turn left in front of a van because you don't see that there could be another car in the other lane and the big van was covering it...and I couldn't even see the little car. It was a good thing I had my seat belt on, or the police said I would not have made it. And this was in 2001. I think that everyone should read this book. There are things that you don't even think about that he is talking about. Insurance companies should discount people that seriously care enough to take this class. It will save lives and accidents.

Marian Chapman Age 76

53

Doodlers from driving class
who liked the teacher
along with the
lessons.

Irenee